Original title:
In the Land of Berries

Copyright © 2025 Creative Arts Management OÜ
All rights reserved.

Author: Zachary Prescott
ISBN HARDBACK: 978-1-80586-278-9
ISBN PAPERBACK: 978-1-80586-750-0

Cobalt Skies and Berry Smiles

Under cobalt skies we laugh and play,
Berries spill out in a wild ballet.
Chasing puddles made by juice's flight,
Laughter echoes from morning to night.

With sticky fingers, we pick and munch,
Every berry's a giggle, a fruity punch.
We wear our snacks like crowns on our heads,
Watching the world, our laughter spreads.

Sun-kissed Fields of Delight

Through sun-kissed fields we skip and roam,
Bouncing like berries, we feel at home.
Every bush holds a treasure, we'd bet,
Surprises await us, in every set.

Grinning from ear to ear with our finds,
Sugar-laced mischief, we leave behind.
We tripped on vines, oh what a show,
The berries all whispered, 'Look at us go!'

Cradled in the Canopy

In the canopy, secrets dance and twirl,
Berry birds gossip in a feathered swirl.
Sneaking snacks from the leafy yonder,
We giggle aloud, it's a berry wonder!

Nestled in branches, we munch with glee,
The fruit of our labor, oh, what a spree!
Tickles from vines, we're soaring high,
Swinging and laughing under the sky.

A Mosaic of Flora and Fruit

In a mosaic of colors, we jump and cheer,
Each berry a buddy, so close and dear.
Mixing and matching, our laughter blends,
Creating a canvas that never ends.

With splattered juice on our clothes, we pose,
Like art on a canvas, we nobody knows.
In this funny garden, we sing out loud,
Where berries and humor make us so proud.

Garden of Sweet Lullabies

Beneath the sun, they wiggle and shake,
Tiny critters dance with a berry cake.
A strawberry giggles, a raspberry sighs,
While blueberries tell jokes, oh what a surprise!

Each fruit holds a secret, a laugh or a snack,
Cherries throw whispers, they never hold back.
The garden hums softly, like a sweet lull,
As plump grapes join in for a fruity hullabaloo!

Twilight's Gathering of Juices

At dusk the berries twinkle, like stars overhead,
Juggling their juices, they lighten the thread.
A lemon jokes loudly, a peach starts to dance,
While oranges giggle, enjoying the chance!

With shadows and laughter, they mix and they swirl,
A raspberry crowns the top of the whirl.
The twilight brigade, so fruity and bright,
Paints the sky yellow, a hilarious sight!

Nets of Flavor

In nets made of laughter, the flavors are caught,
A tangle of berries, the juiciest lot.
Mischievous grapes try to roll off the rack,
While blackberries giggle, giving hints of their snack.

The flavors all flirt, in a fruity parade,
A cherry called out, "Hey! Don't be afraid!"
With puns and with giggles, they weave through the air,
In nets of pure joy, it's a flavor affair!

A Cartography of Sweetness

On maps drawn in jelly, the pathways are fun,
Blueberries lead on, a sweet juicy run.
Raspberries doodle, with squiggly lines,
While lemons draw arrows, making sweet signs.

The puns are laid out, in a grid of delight,
With strawberries giggling, they glow in the night.
Every turn holds a chuckle, each mile a treat,
In this map of yum, adventure's so sweet!

Songbirds Among the Blossoms

Amid the flowers, birds do sing,
Flapping wings, a joyful fling.
Pecking seeds with silly grace,
They dance around, a feathered race.

Chirps and twirls, a merry spree,
One steals berries, oh what glee!
With tiny beaks, they pluck and play,
Making art in the soft sunlight's ray.

The Chase for Plum Perfection

Round and round the branches sway,
Bouncing friends in bright bouquet.
One spots plums, a tempting tease,
But a squirrel swipes them with such ease!

A chase ensues, what a wild race,
Through bushes, trees, a frantic pace.
"You can't catch me!" the squirrel shouts,
As berry lovers spin about.

Berries and Shadows at Dusk

As the sun dips low and fades,
Silly shadows dance on glades.
Berries whisper secret tales,
Of chubby cheeks and sweet, plump trails.

Laughter echoes through the night,
A raccoon sneaks in for a bite.
"Not so fast!" the berries cheer,
As juicy laughter fills the sphere.

A Portrait of Nature's Treats

With every berry, nature boasts,
Tiny treasures, sweetest hosts.
A child with fingers stained in red,
Paints a masterpiece, and then he fled.

A plump blue one rolls away,
"Oh no, catch it!" friends do say.
With giggles echoing through the trees,
They chase that berry on the breeze.

Whispers of the Berry Thicket

Berries giggle on the vine,
They tease the bees, 'Come taste our wine!'
A thief in green with sticky hands,
Shouts, 'I'm king of fruit-filled lands!'

Under leaves where sunlight peeks,
The plump ones blush, the shy one squeaks.
Squirrels scold and chase around,
As berry bonanzas hit the ground!

Rhapsody of Sweet Summer Fruits

Juicy jests in a sunny groove,
Plumping up in their berry move.
Cherries chuckle, blueberries play,
'Let's roll ourselves into a parfait!'

A strawberry sings with a berry lilt,
'We'll bake a pie, no need for guilt!'
Lemons laugh, 'We'll steal the show!'
As oranges juggle, stealing the glow!

The Secret Orchard's Embrace

Hidden gems beneath branches sway,
'Who's gonna find me?' they giggle and play.
Ripe raspberries make a game of hide,
While grapes form a train, rolling wide!

Lurking under the leafy quilt,
Mischief stirs, and the sweetness is built.
Cider fountains burst with joy,
Every sip's a sip-time toy!

Dance of the Crimson Harvest

Berries pirouette like stars at night,
Dancing in baskets, oh what a sight!
Egg on each other with winks and cheers,
'We're the snack that brings the smiles and cheers!'

A toast with jam, we'll spread the fun,
It's a berry bash—let's dance, everyone!
Crispy crusts and toppings galore,
Who knew fruit could make us roar?

Savoring the Wild Essence

Fluffy squirrels gambling, chasing their tails,
A chorus of giggles, where mischief prevails.
Red juice drips down, oh what a sight,
Those berries keep bursting with every bite.

Wobbly knees scramble, oh the delight,
Tasting the sunshine, pure sweetness in flight.
Sticky fingers waving, in playful cheer,
The laughter resounds, summoning friends near.

The Portrait of Juicy Abundance

Canvas of colors, splashes so bright,
Nature's confetti, a fruity delight.
Brush strokes of sweetness, each berry's a star,
Painting my palate, oh how bizarre!

Strings of giggles echo, while tummies do rumble,
All for the perfect, juicy fumble.
Messy and merry, oh what a feast,
This wild masterpiece never to cease.

Orchard Spirits and Summer Dreams

Ghosts of flavors dance, swirling around,
In edible bliss, we're joyfully bound.
The sun winks down, giving us cheer,
With every bright bite, there's nothing to fear.

Dizzy from laughter, we twirl and we spin,
Spirits of summer, it's a fun way to win.
Each berry a giggle, each sip a delight,
As we munch on the magic from morning till night.

Fleeting Moments of Floral Feasting

Petals and laughter twine on the breeze,
Fleeting the moments, oh do as you please.
Chatters and chuckles in full bloom,
A berry banquet, dispelling all gloom.

Tickling our noses, the sweetest bouquet,
In nature's good graces, we frolic and play.
Hands full of fruit, hearts light as air,
In the chaos of joy, what a glorious affair!

Twilight's Berry Bounty

Underneath a wobbly tree,
Berries giggle, feeling free.
A squirrel juggles, what a sight,
His acorn hat is quite the plight!

A bear in shades, wow, what a tease,
Chomping berries with such ease.
He wears a cape, looks like a star,
But trips on roots – oh, there's the scar!

Raccoons craft a berry stew,
With rubber gloves, they're chefs, it's true.
A pie fight starts, oh what a mess,
Berry-covered, they still confess!

As twilight falls, they raise their glass,
To silly fruit—they toast with sass.
Underneath the moon's soft glow,
They laugh and dance, what a berry show!

Echoes of Summer's Feast

Amid grass tall, the berries bloom,
A blueberry's hat? A wild costume!
Strawberries prance, their seeds all bare,
With a berry dance, they spin with flair!

A chorus of ants sings loud and clear,
"Berry bus!" is what we hear.
Raspberries raving, oh, what a thrill,
They plan a party on the hill!

A picnic spread with berries galore,
But the ants sneak in, what a chore!
They bring their friends, and soon you see,
A berry bash, where all agree!

With pies and jokes and laughter bright,
The summer feast continues night.
Each berry tells a tale so sweet,
In this fruity world, we cannot beat!

The Dance of Scarlet Seeds

Beneath the sun where strawberries sway,
The seeds jitterbug, come what may.
A picnic blanket flies on by,
And all the berries start to sigh!

A wild raspberry whispers, 'Hey!
Let's start a dance that steals the day!'
With wiggly roots and jiggly stems,
They form a conga line with gems!

A merry blueberry breaks the mold,
Twirling, swirling, oh so bold!
'We're fruits of joy!' they giggle loud,
As butterflies gather, drawn by the crowd.

As shadows stretch, they take their bows,
Swapping tales with rhymes and hows.
The dance may end, but hearts still race,
In this berry land, we find our place!

Ripe with Promise

In the corner plot, a berry patch,
Promises bloom with every snatch.
A gnome with glasses, quite the chap,
Steals a berry, then takes a nap!

The elder bushes plot their schemes,
As squirrels steal each other's dreams.
A rumor spreads, 'The berries speak!'
'They gossip sweetly, but often squeak!'

'Let's paint our shells in shades of fun!'
Chanted blueberries, 'One for all, all for one!'
With tiny brushes and sticky glee,
They dress up bright, oh, can't you see?

But when it rains, they roll and slide,
Wobbling fruits dance, they're filled with pride.
From spring's first bloom to autumn's cheer,
In this berry patch, all hearts draw near!

Colors of the Hidden Grove

Bright hues laugh beneath the sun,
Each berry hides, a tasty pun.
Oh, the red ones wink and tease,
While purple dreams dance in the breeze.

Green ones giggle, caught in a chase,
Orange shouts, "Come join the race!"
Yellow's sly, holds secrets tight,
As blue ones roll, what a silly sight!

Let's gather all, a feast of cheer,
With fruity jokes and giggles near.
Berry buddies, come take a seat,
In this grove, nothing's discreet!

So swing and sway with berry flair,
Leave your worries, shed your care.
A splash of joy in every bite,
In this grove, we laugh all night!

The Festival of Luscious Temptations

Hats made of leaves for all who dare,
Join the feast, an orchard fair!
Strawberries juggling, on parade,
While raspberry jesters dance, unafraid.

Sweets on sticks, oh what a sight,
A blueberry pie flies through the night!
Peachy pranks and cherry cheers,
Fruity laughter fills our ears.

Berries bounce, a vibrant race,
Watch out, or you'll lose your place!
Take a whiff, the scent's divine,
Daring you to taste the line.

So raise a toast to juicy fun,
Under the glow of the yellow sun.
Break out in laughter, sing and play,
In this festival, come what may!

Tales From the Berry-laden Fields

Once a berry dreamed of flight,
It hopped and rolled into the night.
Raspberry tales of mighty fears,
Soldiers of jam have shed no tears.

Currants waged a war of laughs,
With blueberry knights and silly gaffs.
Strawberry plots, so brightly spun,
Who knew battles could be such fun?

A great parade of berry might,
Filled with mischief, sheer delight.
Marshmallow clouds and fondant skies,
As berry folklore surely flies!

So gather round, let's weave a tale,
Of berry dreams that never fail.
In fields of frolic, let's delight,
With each story, hearts take flight!

The Aroma of Midday Bliss

Whiffs of sweetness fill the air,
Berries frolic, without a care.
Time to nibble, let's embark,
On a journey through this luscious park.

Giggly scents will lead the way,
As berry munchkins laugh and play.
A drizzle here, a sprinkle there,
Lemonade giggles everywhere!

Cherries chat with grassy glee,
As pickles join in merrily.
Wobble and wobble with berry juice,
Fruity frolics, what's the use?

Oh, the jam made laughter swell,
Each taste a story we must tell.
In the midday sun, we roam and sing,
With berry joy, the heart's best fling!

The Crimson Trail

In a land where red splatters,
And juice may leave your shirt,
I tripped on berries scattered,
And laughed till I was hurt.

The bushes whispered secrets,
Of laughter in the air,
I picked with wild abandon,
And stole a berry fair.

With every squished surprise,
A giggle would erupt,
My fingers all sticky,
And my tummy, fully stuffed.

But when the storms did gather,
And clouds began to frown,
Those berries, once a giggle,
Were now my running down!

Raspberry Rhapsody

Oh, the berries dance and twirl,
With a jig that makes me giggle,
The raspberries in their whirl,
They send me into wiggles.

With one big scoop and slurp,
I lost my balance quick,
The sweet burst made me chirp,
And down I went with a flick.

Their laughter fills the air,
As I roll through the patch,
The flavor brings a flare,
A berry-loving match!

Each ripe one that I munch,
Sends my senses aflame,
And in this berry brunch,
It's fun to play the game!

Blue Fragments in a Green World

Amid the leafy splendor,
Blue gems hide with a laugh,
I found myself an ender,
Of a berry-hungry path.

I plucked a berry bold,
And squashed it on my face,
The taste was very cold,
In this berry-flavored race!

Chasing blues with delight,
I tripped on mossy floor,
The fruit showered in flight,
And laughter filled the score.

Though smeared in blueberry bliss,
I wouldn't trade a thing,
For mishaps can't dismiss,
The joy that berry brings!

Tasting the Forest's Heart

Among the trees I wander,
Where the wild things hide, for sure,
I found a berry blunder,
In a bush that's quite obscure.

With a mischievous grin,
I took a tiny bite,
The flavors jumped right in,
And made my taste buds light!

But the stinging bugs did swarm,
As I danced in berry glee,
Each swat a silly form,
Of my forest jubilee.

Now sticky, sore, and spry,
I'll cherish this wild spree,
For with each berry high,
There's a giggle just for me!

Revelry in Raspberry Breezes

In fields where red fruits laugh and sway,
Tiny critters join the berry ballet.
With sticky fingers, joy takes flight,
A fruity fiesta, oh what a sight!

The jam jars tremble in sweet delight,
As ants form bands under the moonlight.
With giggles and splashes, we dive right in,
To berry-picking chaos, let the fun begin!

For every bite, a chuckle shared,
Under the sun, no one is scared.
We toss and tumble, a red-stained spree,
Who knew such fun could come from a tree?

Jelly-fingered friends, what a crew,
Silly faces, berry-covered too.
With laughter echoing through the grove,
We dance and jive, joy's our treasure trove!

Crescendo of Nature's Gems

In a chorus of colors, the fruits appear,
With each juicy note, we break out in cheer.
Blueberries jitter, while strawberries grin,
A symphony of sweetness, let the feast begin!

With tickles and giggles, we gather the hues,
Tomatoes are blushing with shades of bright blues.
A fruit-fueled frenzy, in this joyous choir,
Who knew such splendor could spark such desire?

Under the sunlight, we play hide and seek,
Among vines and branches, the berries peek.
We dance in the grass, as butterflies swoop,
Creating a ruckus in this fruity loop!

Capping off fun with a yogurt swirl,
A berry bonanza in a dizzying whirl.
Laughter's the tune that rings through the day,
With nature's gems, we could laugh and play!

The Gathering of Sweet Memories

A picnic blanket spread, with goods galore,
Giggling friends arrive, there's always room for more.
Berries in baskets, like jewels they gleam,
Sharing sweet moments, living the dream!

We munch on ripe fruits, oh what a sight,
As birds prance above in the warm sunlight.
The juice drips down, and cheeks start to stain,
With laughter and jokes, we dance in the rain!

Sticky embrace, as we relish the day,
The berries may shine, but we steal the hay.
In this raucous gathering, memories form,
Of jelly-flecked noses and friendship's warm charm!

As sunset beckons, we sigh with content,
In a whirlwind of laughter, our hearts are bent.
With every sweet bite, a tale on replay,
A flavorful journey that won't fade away!

Beneath the Boughs' Abundance

Beneath leafy canopies, we take our stand,
With an army of berries, all ripe and grand.
Mischievous laughter fills the sunny air,
As we pluck and proclaim: 'This bounty, we share!'

The squirrels roll by in a berry-fueled chase,
We stumble and tumble, such joy on our face.
With blushing cheeks, we laugh in the breeze,
Who knew berry picking could bring us to knees?

A riot of splendor in colors so bright,
Squirrels in tuxedos, dancing with delight.
We sip on sweet smoothies 'til the sun goes down,
And wear berry crowns like a fruity brown gown!

As dusk settles in, we gather our loot,
With berry-drenched smiles, and oh, what a hoot!
Our harvest of memories fills hearts with glee,
In this orchard of laughter, forever we'll be!

Whimsy Among the Bushes

A squirrel danced upon a vine,
Wearing shoes that were too fine.
He tripped and tumbled down with glee,
Shouting, 'Look at me, I'm free!'

The berries giggled in the sun,
Swaying side to side just for fun.
The ants threw a party, kicked up their feet,
While ladybugs strummed to a tiny beat.

A robin tried to steal the show,
By wearing a hat made of the best dough.
But the berries called, 'Not so fast, my friend!'
And rolled away, their laughter did blend.

So here's to the laughs among the green,
Where silliness reigns, and joy is seen.
With every giggle that bursts like bubble,
Life is a dance—just forget the trouble!

Harvest Moon Over Orchard Dreams

Under a moon of orange hue,
The pumpkins wore pajamas too.
They twirled 'til dawn, oh what a sight,
And said, 'Can you dance? Come join the night!'

The apples joked of a pie so grand,
While pears played tag, as the moonlight spanned.
The owls hooted a goofy tune,
Complaining softly, 'Where's my spoon?'

The shadows twisted, giggled, spun,
As critters joined in, everyone.
With each silly leap, the stars would sway,
Laughing together, till break of day.

So on this night, in the orchard's gleam,
Let's bask in laughter and chase our dreams.
For when the moon shines so bright above,
Every fruit tells tales of joy and love.

The Garden of Lucent Bursts

In a garden where mischief grows,
The carrots wear socks and striking poses.
The peppers giggled in hues so bright,
As daisies twirled in pure delight.

The radishes played hide and seek,
While beets blushed a rosy peek.
A sunflower declared, 'I am the king!'
And called for a crown made of string.

Gnomes threw a party with sparkling juice,
While wiggle-worms danced, oh what a ruse!
The lettuce laughed, 'Join in the cheer!'
For every veggie holds a story dear.

So share a toast with our leafy friends,
In this garden where laughter never ends.
For in every bloom, a chuckle can burst,
Bringing smiles that blossom and quenching thirst.

Violets in their Berry Cloaks

Violets wrapped in berry gowns,
Played dress-up games, twirled around towns.
They painted snails with phrases bright,
While gossiping under the moonlight.

The clouds joined in with fluffy laughs,
As the berries indulged in fruity baths.
'This blueberry's a comedian so wild,'
Said the raspberry, grinning like a child.

They juggled seeds and tossed the sprout,
Each time, a little berry shout!
Nothing was serious, nothing so grim,
In the cloak of fun, they all could swim.

With every blossom, the laughter grew,
In a world where the silly feels so true.
So sway and dance with every note,
For joy is the best berry to promote!

The Berry Gatherer's Lament

Oh, I tripped on a root so bold,
A basket flipped, my treasures rolled.
Sweet juices splattered my face like paint,
A berry thief? This vine's a saint!

With fingers stained as purple as night,
I waved hello to a startled sprite.
He gobbled the goods and disappeared fast,
Was he my friend or just a wild past?

I crouched down low, as sneaky as a fox,
While dodging the bugs that danced on my socks.
A shrub whispered secrets of flavors divine,
Yet all that I'd found was me and this vine!

In my berry dreams, I thought I was slick,
But ended up caught in a sticky old trick.
Next year I'll wear shoes that don't squish,
And maybe share berries with sprite, if I wish!

A Mosaic of Tangles and Flavors

One vine led to another, what a sight,
I thought I was wise, but oh, I was slight.
The berries were bold, the colors so bright,
But I got trapped in a thicket of plight!

The blue ones whispered secrets of cheer,
While reds promised joy and a slice of good beer.
A dance with a thorn bush became my new game,
'Twas berry collecting, but who's really to blame?

With tangles of green wrapping round my head,
I shouted, "Help!" but the bushes just said,
"Keep gathering sweethearts and forget who you are,
You'll be the silliest berry queen by far!"

At last, in the mess, a treasure I spied,
Packed in a jar with a seal so snide.
The label proclaimed it "Best Berry Jam",
But I'm convinced it's just big ol' spam!

Wandering Souls Among the Vines

A couple of friends with empty tummies,
Vowed to find berries, but got too gummy.
We wandered in circles, giggling like kids,
Forgetting our goal, and just rolling like lids!

One climbed a bush, and the other fell down,
I doubled over, with laughter, not frown.
The berries observed—oh what a show!
These wandering souls, well, they didn't quite know!

We gleefully sampled what's ripe in our quest,
With each crazy bite, we thought we were blessed.
But our bellies now heavy, and faces all stained,
We realized too late—we'd over-obtained!

So we settled together upon the sweet ground,
Loudly declaring, "These berries abound!"
Our friendship like fruit, so silly and fine,
These moments of laughter, forever entwined!

The Taste of Forgotten Seasons

In the shade of the branches, I made my own snack,
Fruits that were wrinkly brought laughter, not lack.
I chewed on a berry, sour as my old socks,
But every endearing taste came from rocks!

The seasons were lost, like socks in the wash,
I mused on the fruit while hearing a squosh.
"Is that a cherry or gnome's tiny nose?"
Who knew? The confusion only grows!

With my shirt as a pouch, I gathered my finds,
But with every red berry, I lost my mind.
Chasing down flavors that danced like a sprite,
Oh, the chaos of fruit got me laughing all night!

Fruits like a riddle, a jester's delight,
Each bite brought a giggle—such pure, silly fright.
Adventures in taste that I'll never forget,
In the wild berry world, there's no need to fret!

The Fiesta of Plump Offerings

A jolly bunch of fruit, oh what a sight,
Round and bright, they dance in delight.
Blue is the joker, red takes the lead,
While green holds a laugh, planting a seed.

The festival's here, let's all take a bite,
Jumps and jives, oh what a night!
Raspberry wigs and a cherry parade,
Bananas in sunglasses, aren't they made?

Juicy giggles, oh how they roll,
Strawberries tiptoe, they steal the whole show.
Each berry laughing, wearing a grin,
A cheeky fiesta where all join in!

With pies and tarts, the fun doesn't stop,
Mirth and sweetness, they reach for the top.
The ripest of humor in every berry spin,
In the hilarious dance, let the feast begin!

Shadows of the Blooming Canes.

In a field of canes, where shadows play,
Tall tales are spun at the close of day.
A rascal raspberry whispers a joke,
While giggling green vines make the blossoms poke.

You'd think they're shy, but oh, what a row,
A raspberry riddle, who knows how?
The shadows grow long, but spirits don't fade,
In this wacky world where pranks are made.

A wandering berry trips on its flank,
Laughing it off, it wanders the bank.
Swinging sweet stories, they bounce and twirl,
As the sun dips low and the dreams unfurl.

One last chuckle before they must sleep,
These musical fruits have secrets to keep.
In shadows so silly, the laughter will stay,
While the blooms remain merry, in their quirky play!

Whispers of Wild Harvest

Nestled in brambles, the secrets do chirp,
A blueberry peeks, with a humorous burp.
Gather 'round friends, it's time for a feast,
With jolly old fruits, the laughter won't cease.

Out in the wild, mischief abounds,
A merry old strawberry spins round and rounds.
Tickling the bushes, making them sway,
These fruits know how to brighten the day!

Grab a basket, let's fill it with cheer,
Each berry a joker, their antics sincere.
As the harvest rolls in, watch the grape juggle,
With giggles and grins, there's never a struggle.

Whispers of sweetness dance on the breeze,
A band of wild folks who do as they please.
With jokes and with joy, they savor the fun,
For the wild is alive when the picking's begun!

Sweetness Beneath the Thicket

Under the thicket, where stories collide,
A berry brigade has nothing to hide.
With a wink and a laugh, they roll down the hill,
In a contest for sweetness, they just can't stand still.

Oh the mischief they brew, with laughter so loud,
A raspberry giggles, proud in the crowd.
Jumping from bushes, such silly displays,
Chasing their shadows in whimsical plays.

The sweetness is ripe, and the jokes are too,
Bananas in costumes, who knew they could do?
Mirthful mayhem beneath leafy strands,
Tickled and twisted by nature's own hands.

So gather your pals, let the thicket unite,
In a frenzy of laughter, a truly sweet sight.
These fruits hold a party, a carnival bright,
Where the joy of the harvest ignites the night!

The Harvested Rainbow

A plant dressed up in spots of red,
Where jellybeans might fear to tread.
The squirrels debate which fruit to pick,
While raccoons plot their evening trick.

A tasting party beneath the trees,
With fruit punch spills and giggling bees.
The sunlight dances on sticky hands,
As laughter echoes across the lands.

Berry hats are worn with pride,
While pirates seek treasures inside.
Each bite a burst, a sweet delight,
In a feast that lasts well into the night.

So grab a cup, fill it high,
And toast to the moon in the berry sky.
With every sip, a giggle flows,
In this fruity land, where fun just grows.

Beneath the Bough of Abundance

Underneath the leafy dome,
Where berry bandits call it home.
The fruits argue, 'Who's the best?'
While whispers challenge every jest.

Blueberries boast a royal flair,
While raspberries flaunt their vibrant hair.
The strawberries giggle, plump with cheer,
As ants parade with nothing to fear.

A fruit fight brews, oh what a sight!
With juice and jam, they take to flight.
Each laugh is ripe, each pun is sweet,
In this cheeky dance, no one's discreet.

So gather round, bring your flair,
And let's make chaos without a care.
For under this bough, we're free to roam,
In this wacky patch, we find our home.

Unraveling the Berry Tapestry

A woven tale of red and blue,
Where every berry has a view.
They gather round, they share their lore,
In this sweet saga, who could ask for more?

The grape antics draw the crowd,
Its stories lively, bold, and loud.
And when the blackberries tell a joke,
The bushes rumble, and laughter stokes.

Farmer's hat and mud-laden feet,
Dance with rhythm to this zesty beat.
With sticky fingers and cherry stains,
We revel in this berry reign.

So let's yarn tales of fruit divine,
With every giggle, let the juice align.
Each twist a flavor, each turn a game,
In this berry world, we dance untamed.

The Dancers of Sweet Wine and Sunlight

The sun spills laughter on the vine,
Where grapes pretend to sip on wine.
Each clump a troupe, a vibrant show,
Performing steps that steal the glow.

Peaches rolling with rhymes so sweet,
Waltz down paths on joyful feet.
They twirl and spin, a fruity spree,
As bees provide the harmony.

A jester berry juggles well,
While cherries giggle, their stories swell.
The melon casts a shadow wide,
Inviting all to come inside.

So let's raise glasses with berry cheer,
To this fruity fandango, far and near.
With every sip, we tap our feet,
In this bubbling bliss, we find our beat.

The Taste of Forgotten Seasons

Once I chomped a berry bright,
Thought it was pure delight.
But the taste, oh what a fight,
Left my tummy feeling tight.

In the bush, they danced with glee,
Mocking me from every tree.
They knew I'd take a spree,
But left me with a big "Whoopsie!"

Each bite a twist and turn,
My taste buds start to burn.
I learned that berries churn,
A lesson best to spurn.

So here's to seasons gone,
With berries I forlorn.
I'll stick to cake and moan,
And leave those fruits alone!

An Ode to Nature's Sweetness

Oh, the round and jolly fruits,
Plump like tiny veggie boots!
Ate one and thought, "How cute!"
Ended up chasing squirrels in suits.

With squishy bites and sticky hands,
Nature's joke, no one understands.
Juice stains mark my dance plans,
As I slip through berry bands.

Each berry's a laugh in disguise,
With flavors that twist and rise.
Sour, sweet, a weird surprise,
Leaves me giggling 'til I cry.

So here's to nature's fun treat,
With each berry, funny feet!
May my laughter never deplete,
As I prance on fruity beat!

Fields of Color, Fields of Flavor

In fields where colors collide,
Berries drop like joy, bonafide.
I burst through bushes with pride,
But oh, what's this? A berry slide!

Rolling down like nature's balls,
Laughing at my berry falls.
In this land, the fun enthralls,
While I end up stuck in stalls.

Green, red, and purple parade,
Chasing flavors that invade.
But watch out for the berry raid,
Nature laughs as plans are made.

So here we go, let's taste and cheer,
While berries giggle year to year.
The sweetness pulls us near,
In fields of color, we show no fear!

Gathering Nature's Jewels

With baskets wide, we roam around,
Picking gems from the ground.
But berries, sly, they've all found,
A way to dodge—such clever hound!

Look at that one, oh what a tease!
Dodging fingers with such ease.
Juicy jokes among the trees,
Nature's prankster, if you please.

When I thought I'd score a win,
The berry's laughter, oh so thin,
"Try again, my friend, begin!"
While I just smirk and grin.

With a laugh and squishy hands,
I gather more, despite their plans.
For nature's sweets, my heart expands,
As joy in berry form withstands!

Blooming Expectations

A patch of red, so bold and bright,
The critters gather, what a sight!
They dream of pies, oh what a tease,
But step in quick, or you'll get fleeced!

The berries giggle, they roll and sway,
Quick! Grab a basket, don't delay!
The fruit flies dive, the ants parade,
In this wild race, don't be dismayed.

With silly hats and messy hands,
They munch on snacks like happy bands.
The juice, it splatters, laughter flows,
Who knew that fruit could steal the show?

So join the fun, come take a bite,
But watch your step—what a delight!
With every berry, a silly cheer,
Oh, such sweet chaos, year after year!

The Heartbeat of the Orchard

In shadows dance the jolly crew,
Plotting schemes of berry stew.
The trees chuckle, the bushes sigh,
As laughter blooms beneath the sky.

Each plump delight, a playful tease,
Ready to tempt the hungry bees.
The squirrels plan a berry feast,
While pigeons waddle, not the least!

A squabble breaks, they spill with glee,
A berry juggling symphony!
They tumble in a fruity spree,
Oh look out—it's a fruit jubilee!

With every bite, the giggles grow,
It's berry madness, don't you know?
So dance along, embrace the cheer,
In this orchard, fun's always near!

A Festival of Flavor

Gather round, oh what a scene,
A berry festival, bright and keen!
With blueberry muffins, oh my dear,
A fruity feast that draws us near.

The jam jars line the tables wide,
Strawberry smiles, our hearts collide.
A contest of pies, who'll take the crown?
Watch out, it's about to go down!

Cackle and chatter, trucks roll in,
Flavors will dance and hearts will win!
From raspberry tarts to cherry cheer,
Each bite's a laugh, let's raise a beer!

So pull a friend, share a slice,
In this berry bash, oh isn't it nice?
Joy in every flavor, that's our goal,
At the festival, where good times roll!

Dappled Light and Growing Fruits

Sunbeams filter through the leaves,
Whispering secrets, where joy weaves.
The berries bounce, up high and low,
In this merry game, they steal the show!

The crickets chirp, the laughter rings,
As fruit-filled dreams take flight on wings.
The ground is buzzing, ants parade,
A sillier sight? You're not dismayed!

Each berry glimmers, each vine alive,
Bringing delight as friends arrive.
Smirks and giggles, a funny tune,
Beneath the watch of a cheeky moon.

So gather closely, let joy ignite,
In the dappled glow, everything's bright.
With every bite, a joke we share,
In this fruitful land, without a care!

The Berry Patch Chronicles

In a patch so spry and bright,
Berries bounce, oh what a sight!
One rolled down with all its might,
Claiming it's a berry knight!

Chasing round the quirky vines,
Came a squirrel with silly signs.
He wore a berry crown so fine,
Proclaiming, "I'm the berry line!"

A fox jumped in with berry flair,
Claiming he could dance, beware!
He slipped and slid, gave quite a scare,
We laughed and rolled, no time to care.

At dusk we feasted by the brook,
With berry cakes and funny looks.
We toasted with our berry juice,
And every giggle let loose!

Secrets of the Sunkissed Vines

Underneath the sun so bold,
Hidden gems in reds and gold.
We'd dance about, not caring cold,
For berry stories, we have told.

A bunny hopped with fruity cheer,
Singing loud for all to hear.
"I'm a berry!" he did leer,
His voice, it tickled, oh so near.

A bird flew down to steal a taste,
Made a face, no time to waste!
"These crunchy snacks are far from paste!"
We chuckled hard, our sides embraced.

With laughter ringing through the woods,
We shared our berry-like good moods.
These silly vibes, we all understood,
In the sun, we danced for good!

A Feast for the Senses

The table set with berry treats,
With jelly beans and funky beats.
We danced around with sticky feet,
And nibbled sweets, oh what a feat!

A grumpy old toad croaked a song,
Said berries made him feel so wrong.
But when he tasted, he danced along,
His legs flew high, it won't be long!

Pies piled high with whipped cream towers,
As we munched our fruity flowers.
Laughter echoed in the hours,
Berry bliss with all its powers.

So come and join this tasty game,
With berry giggles, nothing's lame.
Each bite a laugh, never the same,
In this fun patch, we found our fame!

Beneath the Berry Boughs

Beneath the boughs of berry trees,
We swung about and caught the breeze.
A raccoon waved, "Oh, if you please,"
Join us for some berry keys!

A polka-dotted snail slid by,
With tiny shades that caught the eye.
"I'm here for jam!" he said, oh my,
All of us giggled, we couldn't lie.

A hedge of berries without a sound,
Grew secrets, hidden underground.
We unearthed giggles all around,
While berry juice turned our hands brown.

So gather 'round, let's make a cheer,
For berry days we hold so dear.
With funny tales and laughter near,
We'll savor fun, year after year!

Beneath the Canopy of Blue

Under azure skies, we play,
Dancing round in berries' sway.
With laughter sweet, we pick and pluck,
Who knew fruit could bring such luck?

A squishy berry lands on my toe,
Its juicy burst steals the show.
Sticky fingers, giggles fly,
As we munch beneath the sky.

The sunbeams wink, they feel the zest,
Each berry hints at a funny quest.
With every bite, a tale is spun,
Our silly games have just begun.

Beneath this vast and sunny dome,
We find a wild and tasty home.
In berry bliss, we romp and roam,
With silly seeds, we'll never moan.

The Lure of Juicy Dreams

A berry throne, a king's delight,
Where flavors burst and dreams take flight.
With marshmallow clouds and jelly rains,
We chase the sweetness, lose our pains.

Squeezed between two juicy treats,
Our giggles mix with sticky eats.
The fruit parade must never end,
It's a banquet shared with every friend.

With grape-stained smiles, we make a pact,
To chomp and chew, not miss an act.
Each berry bite, a comedy,
In this wild, fruity symphony.

And as the sun begins to fade,
A trail of laughter marks our raid.
In dreams of berry, we'll entwine,
Forever laughing, feeling fine.

In the Shade of Thorny Bushes

Amidst the thorns, we dare to creep,
A secret space where fruit does leap.
With berry babble and silly sighs,
Each hidden jewel is a sweet surprise.

Watch out for grumpy bushes there,
They poke and prod without a care.
We laugh as we dodge, our challenge set,
For every prick, we won't forget.

The treasure's ripe, the charm is true,
With faces painted in berry goo.
We giggle as we slimy slide,
In this fun mess, we take great pride.

Shadows dance in our berry patch,
Every moment, a new fun match.
With friendship bright, our spirits soar,
In thorny shade, who could ask for more?

Heartstrings of the Berry Patch

Each berry picked, a giggle shared,
With friends around, we're never scared.
Juicy hearts in laughter mixed,
Our berry bond can't be unfixed.

With splashes of juice, we create a scene,
Where every berry's a clown, so keen.
Slipping and sliding, we fall in a heap,
In this patch of joy, no time for sleep.

Tickled by leaves and sweet delight,
Our sunny days stretch into night.
We strum on vines, a funny tune,
The berry patch sings beneath the moon.

So let's toast to laughter, loud and clear,
In the sweetness of fruit, we've got no fear.
With hearts wide open, we make our mark,
In this berry land, we'll always spark.

A Berrylicious Adventure

In a patch where smiles gleam,
Plump fruits bounce, a playful dream.
Rabbits snicker, squirrels race,
Laughing berries fill the space.

Under sun that tickles skin,
A jam-making contest to begin.
Who'll squish the squishiest treat?
Berry juice is quite the feat!

Cakes and pies, oh what a sight,
Dancing fruits, a pure delight.
With each bite, giggles wane,
Berry munching is never plain!

Flavors burst like silly jokes,
Fruits whisper, giggle, poke.
In their world, we take a stand,
Berry fun is always grand!

Reflections on a Fruitful Day

Sunrise calls with fruity cheer,
To pick the best and have no fear.
Each berry holds a secret smile,
Wearing sweetness all the while.

A basket heavy, dreams afloat,
Bouncing round in a silly boat.
Frogs play chess, the ants conspire,
While I munch on berry fire.

Tickled by the insistent breeze,
I talk to plants, they giggle, tease.
A berry pie becomes my muse,
With cream and sugar, how could I lose?

At dusk, the laughter swirls in air,
Berries whisper tales to share.
In reflections of this splendid stay,
I grin at all the berry play!

The Language of Blossoms

Petals wave like tiny flags,
Berries bounce, they play, they wag.
Roses gossip, daisies chuckle,
While fruit delights in its own shuffle.

Whispers low in golden light,
Berries blush in sheer delight.
They speak in flavors, sweet and bold,
Every taste, a tale retold.

A strawberry winks, a raspberry grins,
Blackberries giggle, feeling wins.
Cherries strut in their shiny red,
While blueberries burst like thoughts in my head.

Nature's jesters, it's no surprise,
Fruits dance under open skies.
In their laughter, flowers sway,
A joyful language at play!

Evocations of Berry Flavors

Sweetness drips from every vine,
Berries plucked with giggles fine.
Taste buds wander, explore the scene,
In this fruity realm, we're kings and queens.

Lemonade laughs, oh so zesty,
Berries bounce, feeling festy.
Every sip ignites a cheer,
Berry magic, crystal clear.

Pie crusts crack with berry delight,
Inside them, giggles take flight.
Each morsel sings the sweetest sound,
In every bite, joy is found.

Under stars, we share our dreams,
Fruity laughter, giggly schemes.
With flavors swirling in a dance,
In berry bliss, we find our chance!

Beneath the Canopy of Delights

Underneath the leafy green,
A berry dance, a wobbly scene.
Birds are chirping, squirrels flirt,
While I trip on my own shirt!

Lemonade falls from above,
Nature's gift, so sweet and tough.
Giggles rise with each new find,
But oh, the ants, they're quite unkind!

Laughter bubbles from the brook,
While I squeeze a pickle's nook.
Fruits are bouncing, oh so spry,
Who knew veggies could fly high?

In this realm of silly cheer,
Candy worms that disappear.
Such a jolly, odd parade,
All the puzzling games we've played!

A Serenade in Berry Hues

Fiddlers play on berry vines,
While I juggle jars of brines.
Blue and red, they dance around,
As I stumble on the ground!

Muffins having a grand feast,
Cupcakes laughing, not the least.
Cherries wear their sassy hats,
Dancing with the silly rats!

Strawberry kings and peachy queens,
Throwing pies at silly scenes.
Watch those berries bounce and soar,
Leaving sweet crumbs on the floor!

In this funny berry bliss,
Each fruit smiles, can't resist.
So let's twirl, and let it show,
A fruity world where giggles flow!

The Hidden Pathway to Sweetness

Through the bushes, oh so bright,
A hidden path, a pure delight.
Muffin tops wear sassy grins,
While cookie jars hold secret wins!

Berry bushes hide their prize,
With juicy truths and silly lies.
Every step brings feathery friends,
While the laughter never ends!

Chasing shadows, what a thrill,
Found a berry on the hill.
It's pretending to be blue,
But really? It's a fruit stew!

Beneath the giggles, funny cheers,
A berry tale through all the years.
So come along and take a peek,
At antics that will make you squeak!

Palettes of Nature's Palette

Colors splash across the field,
Every hue a joke revealed.
Purple socks on pickle feet,
Making tracks where berries meet!

Feathered friends in berry hats,
Chasing tails of goofy cats.
Painted skies and laughter bright,
Fruits have secrets hid from sight!

Rainbow raindrops giggle down,
As fruitcake wears a jester's crown.
Twirling, swirling in delight,
Every berry sings goodnight!

So grab your brush, and join the fun,
Every laugh beneath the sun.
A colorful, wacky serenade,
In this world, we've all mislaid!

Woven in Natural Threads

A patch of red with a hint of green,
Bouncing berries, a comical scene.
The squirrels are plotting, with secretive glee,
While I dodge their acorns, just trying to flee.

Oops! I tripped on a vine, so spry,
Now my face is a feast for the flies.
The berries chuckle, they know I'm a mess,
In this jungle of laughter, I must confess!

Caught in the web of sweet sticky plight,
Picking too quick, I lost my bite.
With every squished treasure my fingers plead,
I laugh it off, I'm just planting a seed.

Now the birds are playing a mischievous game,
Pecking at fruit, driving me insane.
But in every comical berry fiasco,
I find simple joy in this fruity lasso.

The Youth of Juicy Harvests

A berry brigade, they dance in a row,
Wobbling and jiggling, just put on a show.
One berry whispers, 'I'm ripe for the choice!'
While another chimes in, 'You're not the only voice!'

The ground's so bumpy, I skip and I slide,
These plump little jesters have nowhere to hide.
A berry's bright wink sends me screaming with cheer,
Who knew harvest time brought such giggles near?

With sticky fingers and a grin ear to ear,
I scoop up the laughter, my greatest souvenir.
Each berry's a punchline that begs to be told,
In a world full of humor, I'm never too old.

So let's gather round, and share tales of day,
As we munch on our spoils in a berry ballet.
In the youth of the harvest, joy takes its stand,
With some fruity friends and life's quirky strand.

Speckles of Sunshine

Sunshine drips from the branches above,
Little globes of light, full of giggles and love.
I reach for a handful, bright colors collide,
Each berry a smile, laughter vitally tied.

The rabbits all chuckle, they know they're quite sly,
Making off with my pickings as I wonder why.
A berry slips down and lands on my shoe,
'Join the party!' it giggles, 'We're waiting for you!'

Tickles in my tummy, the humor's alive,
Sneaky little fruits, oh how they contrive!
'Catch me if you can!' shouts a berry so bold,
Chasing their laughter, I feel ten years old.

As the sun starts to set, the jokes keep on flowing,
Nature's own comedy troupe, endlessly glowing.
With speckles of sunshine that lighten the air,
I cherish the moments, free from all care.

Tales from the Sweet Underbrush

In the thicket where antics begin to unwind,
Berries are storytellers, revealing their mind.
A raspberry claims it can dance on a leaf,
While a blueberry giggles, 'That's pure disbelief!'

Underneath shadows, where mischief is rife,
Cherries bicker and argue about their sweet life.
'You think you're the best? Well, wait 'til you see
How I'll steal this show with my maraschino glee!'

Listening close, I can't help but just smile,
These tiny theatrics make life feel worthwhile.
Between all the laughter and berries galore,
I pen all their stories, can't wait for more!

So gather around, dear friends of this patch,
There's tales of adventure, humorous and brash.
In the sweet underbrush, no moment's mundane,
Every fruity giggle, a spark of the insane!

Abundant Whispers of Freshness

Beneath the bush, a furry friend,
Can't resist those treats to send.
A squishy treasure, soft and sweet,
He's got a berry party, can't be beat!

From berry jail, the thrill to escape,
With juicy beads, oh what a shape!
The squirrel snickers, wears a crown,
As berries rain, he'll never frown!

Handfuls gathered, what a haul,
Now to make a trampoline, oh what a call!
Laughter echoes as we bounce along,
With berry juice, we'll sing a song!

The picnic spread laid with care,
Mismatched socks dance in the air.
We toast to the snacks, so round and bright,
With berry smoothies, what a sight!

The Art of Foraging Joy

With baskets swinging, laughter flows,
Who knew the bush would have such pros?
A funny hat, now on my head,
Berries will inspire tales we've read!

One berry squish, then two or three,
I'm met with giggles and a plea.
The dog looks jealous, sits and begs,
Searching for treasures beneath the legs!

Through sticky fingers, we all unite,
With stained shirts, it's such a sight!
Our faces smeared, a berry bliss,
In this fruity chaos, we won't miss!

By sunset's glow, a toast sincere,
With berry pie, let's give a cheer!
In strawberry drama, our tales unfurl,
To celebrate the juiciest world!

Petals and Pints of Berry Bliss

Under petals, laughter fills the air,
Mixing flavors without a care.
Whipped cream clouds above our heads,
As berries dive into chocolate spreads!

Excited squeals, a giggle fest,
Who can resist this fruity quest?
The dog joins in—what a surprise,
With berry stains that match the skies!

Each sip of juice is pure delight,
Bouncing giggles from left to right.
With sticky fingers and brightened smiles,
In this berry wonder, let's stay awhile!

A toast with pints, let's raise them high,
To berry dreams that soar and fly!
We'll sip and laugh by kitchen light,
With every berry, life feels right!

Sun-drenched Trails of Flavor

Golden rays and berry trails,
With chuckles shared, our laughter sails.
A sticky path filled with cheer,
We search for munchies, oh my dear!

One berry, two, and then a splash—
A tiny face turned bright with gash.
Who knew that berries could bring such glee?
As juice drips down, they laugh at me!

A wigs of leaves, a costume grand,
We skip like sprites across the land.
Surprises lurk in every twist,
With berry treasure that can't be missed!

So let's indulge in this fine feast,
With jolly giggles, we'll get released.
The trails of sunshine, oh create,
New berry tales that simply await!

Symphonies of the Wild Delights

In a corner of the grove, where the mishmash grows,
Bouncing berries sing sweetly, just like silly prose.
Squirrels twirl in the breeze, with hats made of leaves,
A party of the critters, as laughter weaves.

Giant strawberries giggle, hiding under a leaf,
While blueberries moonwalk, spreading wild disbelief.
Raspberries are cheeky, throwing seeds like confetti,
In this jolly jubilee, everything's unsteady.

Cherries juggle sunshine, giggling as they sway,
Bouncing off the brambles, in a berry ballet.
As the whispers of the bushes tickle every ear,
Nature's folly is abundant, bursting with good cheer.

In this wacky wonderland, where everything's a jest,
Join the dance of fruity fun, it's just the very best.
From dandelion trumpets to the claps of little ants,
The vines are filled with laughter, in wild berry prance.

Veils of Sun-kissed Rubies

A treasure trove of laughter, where rubies freely shine,
Jellybeans of the forest, all drenched in slight divine.
Pick the jesting jewels, plump and sweet as can be,
While frogs wear crowns of clovers, feeling fancy and free.

Ripe cherries vie for giggles, bouncing in their glee,
With little mice as dancers, oh what a sight to see!
Raspberry vines are tangled, in a merry jigsaw twist,
As all the berry lovers share giggles in the mist.

Sunlight drips like syrup, upon this sugary scene,
As bushy-tailed jesters prance, they're frolicking unseen.
Their antics keep us chuckling, with laughter bright in tow,
In sun-kissed realms of fruity fun, the antics steal the show.

A candy-coated wonder, where mirth is in the air,
Nature's jesters play a tune, spreading joy everywhere.
So dive into this revelry, let your worries float,
Among the berry laughter, you'll find life's little note.

Echoes of Nature's Palette

A palette filled with giggles, splattered wild and bright,
Where the fruity fun and laughter bounce from morning to night.
Each brush of color dances, with cheer beyond compare,
As butterflies join in the chaos, swirling everywhere.

Frogs wear flower crowns, croaking silly tunes,
While berries boil with laughter, under lazy afternoons.
Brush strokes of the sunbeam, dab the leaves with joy,
Nature's art is playful, like a whimsical toy.

Ripe peaches throw confetti, in puffs of fuzzy fluff,
While hedgehogs roll in colors, thinking that's enough.
With every berry blinking, as the creatures share their whims,
The echoes of the palette, ring loud in happy hymns.

So waddle through the wilderness, where hilarity reigns,
Join this feast of fruity fun, let go of all your chains.
For in the vibrant chaos, where laughter finds its spark,
You'll discover nature's wonders, painting happiness in the park.

Nectar Trails in the Twilight

As dusk begins to dance, with a wink from the moon,
The nectar trails are lit, humming a merry tune.
Bumblebees are buzzing jokes, tasty as they fly,
A fruity cabaret unfolds, as night begins to sigh.

The plush plums throw a party, dressed in shades of night,
While fireflies do cha-cha, twinkling with delight.
Juicy pears are giggling, spilling nectar here and there,
And all the critters gather, without a single care.

The stars drip juicy stardust, upon the playful field,
Where laughter shapes the shadows, as the day's joys are revealed.
Each fruit a jolly fellow, in the twilight's gentle hand,
Creating sweet adventure, in this berry-laden land.

So let's toast to the antics, sipped from nature's cup,
With nectar trails of laughter, let's all smile and sup.
In this dreamy escapade, roll in the berry fun,
As night wraps up the treasures, 'til the morning sun.

www.ingramcontent.com/pod-product-compliance
Lightning Source LLC
Chambersburg PA
CBHW070317120526
44590CB00017B/2709